THE
FRIENDSHIP
POEMS
OF
RUMI

Inspiring | Educating | Creating | Entertaining

Brimming with creative inspiration, how-to projects, and useful information to enrich your everyday life, Quarto Knows is a favorite destination for those pursuing their interests and passions. Visit our site and dig deeper with our books into your area of interest: Quarto Creates, Quarto Cooks, Quarto Homes, Quarto Lives, Quarto Drives, Quarto Explores, Quarto Gifts, or Quarto Kids.

First published in 2020 by Wellfleet Press,
an imprint of The Quarto Group,
142 West 36th Street, 4th Floor,
New York, NY 10018, USA
T (212) 779-4972 F (212) 779-6058
www.QuartoKnows.com

Wellfleet titles are also available at discount for retail, wholesale, promotional, and bulk purchase. For details, contact the Special Sales Manager by email at specialsales@quarto.com or by mail at The Quarto Group, Attn: Special Sales Manager, 100 Cummings Center Suite 265D, Beverly, MA 01915 USA.

10 9 8 7 6 5 4 3 2 1

ISBN: 978-1-57715-219-4

Library of Congress Cataloging-in-Publication Data

Names: Jalāl al-Dīn Rūmī, Maulana, 1207-1273, author.
    | Khalīlī, Nādir, translator.
Title: The friendship poems of Rumi / translated by
    Nader Khalili.
Description: New York : Wellfleet Press, 2020. | Series:
    Timeless Rumi | Summary: "The Friendship Poems of
    Rumi is an elegantly illustrated gift book of the famous
    Rumi's poems, translated by Nader Khalili, that center
    on the meaning of friendship and its many beautiful
    meanings"-- Provided by publisher.
Identifiers: LCCN 2020005464 (print) | LCCN
    2020005465 (ebook) | ISBN 9781577152194
    (hardcover) | ISBN 9780760368367 (ebook)
Subjects: LCSH: Jalāl al-Dīn Rūmī, Maulana,
    1207-1273--Translations into English. | LCGFT: Poetry.
Classification: LCC PK6480.E5 K25 2020 (print)
    | LCC PK6480.E5 (ebook) | DDC 891/.5511--dc23
LC record available at https://lccn.loc.gov/2020005464
LC ebook record available at https://lccn.loc.
gov/2020005465

Publisher: Rage Kindelsperger
Creative Director: Laura Drew
Managing Editor: Cara Donaldson
Project Editor: Leeann Moreau
Art Director: Cindy Samargia Laun
Book Design and Illustration: Evelin Kasikov

Printed in China

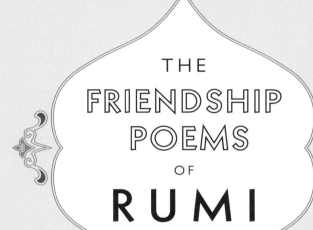

THE
FRIENDSHIP
POEMS
OF
RUMI

Translated by
NADER KHALILI

WELLFLEET
PRESS

CONTENTS

AN INTRODUCTION TO RUMI'S FRIENDSHIP POETRY

Jalaloddin Mohammed Balkhi Rumi was born in 1207, in the city of Balkh, which is in present-day Afghanistan. He and his family fled from invading Mongols and settled in Konya—once a small town, it is now a major Turkish city. He lived the rest of his life there, studying languages, science, logic, and Islamic philosophy. He was a respected Islamic scholar and teacher on a steadfast course until the day he met great upheaval in the form of Shams Tabrizi, a Sufi Master who came to Konya in 1244.

Rumi was drawn to Shams, becoming his student and undergoing a profound transformation. The two spent an abundance of time together philosophizing and conversing until Shams was sent away to Syria, breaking Rumi's heart. Shams came back only to disappear again, this time forever, and this separation was to Rumi a manifestation of divine heartbreak. While he felt pain in separation, he took great joy from union. He knew that while he felt pained, he was never really separate from Shams or God. It was all this love, heartbreak, and longing that turned his soul to poetry.

In his life, he created 65,000 verses, many of which are *robaiyat*, or quatrains. His poems were recorded by his students as he recited them while whirling in the ecstatic dervish dance. The poetry was collected into two books, *Diwan-i Shams-I Tabrizi (The Collected Poetry of Shams)* and *Mathnawi (Spiritual Couplets)*.

Rumi remained a beloved and respected mystic throughout his life, and countless readers today consider him to be the very best Persian poet of his—or any—age. He reached what he called "the roots of the roots of the roots of the divine," meaning that his poetry captures a crucial aspect of Islam, and many other religions, which is that people can find bliss and freedom through pure love.

This collection of his poetry to inspire companionship is gathered from the nonliteral translations of Nader Khalili (see page 128). The poems selected for this volume appear in two parts: (1) *Fountain of Fire* and (2) *Dancing the Flame*, which contain poems chosen from Khalili's books of those same names.

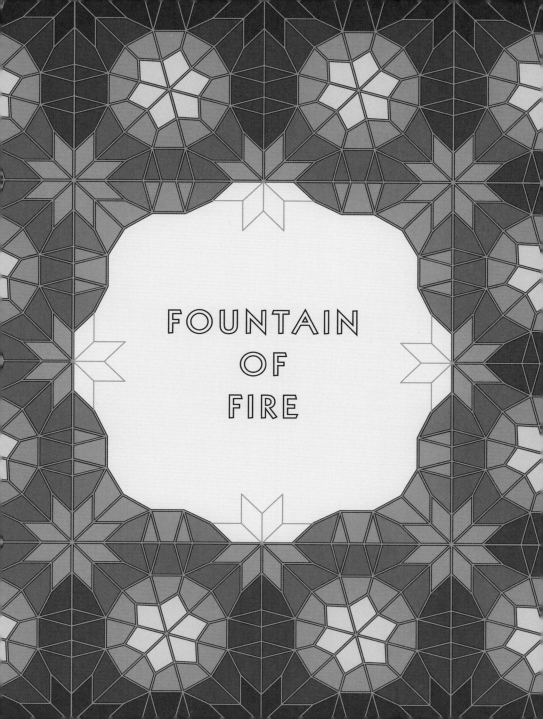

FOUNTAIN
OF
FIRE

COME ON SWEETHEART

come on sweetheart
lets' adore one another
before there is no more
of you and me

a mirror tells the truth
look at your grim face
brighten up and cast away
your bitter smile

a generous friend
gives life for a friend
let's rise above this
animalistic behavior
and be kind to one another

spite darkens friendships
why not cast away
malice from our heart

once you think of me
dead and gone
you will make up with me
you will miss me
you may even adore me

why be a worshipper of the dead
think of me as a goner
come and make up now

since you will come
and throw kisses
at my tombstone later
why not give them to me now
this is me
that same person

i may talk too much
but my heart is silence
what else can i do
i am condemned to live this life

THIS TIME I MUST CONFESS

this time i must confess
i feel a total hate for myself
while crowded and swarmed
my heart wishes to be by single self

seeking that single pearl
i cave to dive deep into this sea
but fear of murderous waves
makes me beg for your help my friends

scattered with so much going on inside
i long for nothing but an inner unity
duality must be abandoned
if you seek to drink the soul of unity

you must bet and lose
everything you've ever owned
if you truly desire
to become one with your beloved

listen to the secret sound
of the revelation now
when your quest aspires the skies
fly away from this lowly earth

my heavenly soul
who only nests in the heights
is tired of its house on earth
it wants to abandon the body
it wants to take the final flight

LOOK WHAT YOU HAVE DONE

look what you have done
hunted my heart
hunted my soul
but left them behind

you raptured my life
broke my cage
but wounded to depart

though i know your wish
though i suffer the separation
i have no courage to ask
what have you done

i know why a candle burns
i know why a candle cries
since you're the cause
of pulling its life apart

i know why a harp
bows as it is played
since like a slave
you made it bend to obey

with all the tyranny you caused
as soon as i see your face
my poisoned life turns sweet
my pain is perfectly healed

every leaf in hope
hold its palm open
begging for more
knowing your endless bliss

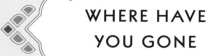

WHERE HAVE YOU GONE

where have you gone
the settler of my soul
did you fly away
or hide in your home

as soon as you saw
the loyalty of my heart
you turned around and
flew like a bird

your vision captured
the wandering of our spirits
then away from the crowd
you journeyed in solitude

you went away so quick
as though you were
a morning breath
carrying a flower's aroma

but you really didn't fly away
as a bird or breeze
you were created from God's light
you went immersed in his glow

FIND YOURSELF
A FRIEND

find yourself a friend
who is willing to
tolerated you with patience

put to the test the essence
of the best incense
by putting it in fire

drink a cup of poison
if handed to you by a friend
when filled with love and grace

step into the fire
like the chosen prophet
the secret love will change
hot flames to a garden
covered with blossoms
roses and hyacinths and willow

spinning and throwing you
a true friend can hold you
like God and his universe

IF YOU STAY AWAKE

if you stay awake
for an entire night
watch out for a treasure
trying to arrive

you can keep warm
by the secret sun of the night
keeping your eyes open
for the softness of dawn

try it for tonight
challenge your sleepy eyes
do not lay your head down
wait for heavenly alms

night is the bringer of gifts
Moses went on a ten year journey
during a single night
invited by a tree
to watch the fire and light

Mohammad too made his passage
during that holy night
when he heard the glorious voice
when he ascended to the sky

day is to make a living
night is only for love
commoners sleep fast
lovers whisper to God all night

all night long
a voice calls you upon you
to wake up
in the precious hours

if you miss
your chance now
your soul will lament
when your body is left behind

COME ON DARLING

come on darling
pass me one more cup
bestow on my soul
tranquility once more

and do it now
today is my turn
i can wait no more
for the unknown tomorrow

if you have as my share
even a small trace of grace
give it to me now
don't make me wait

let me go free
help me to break out
from this new trap
i've fallen into again

don't hand me over
to the monster of my thoughts
my thoughts are another trap
another waiting vampire

take my only belongings
take them to the pawn shop
pledge them once more and
bring me the last cup

DON'T GO TO SLEEP

don't go to sleep
this night
one night is worth
a hundred thousand souls

the night is generous
it can give you
a gift of the full moon
it can bless your soul
with endless treasure

every night when you feel
the world is unjust
never ending grace
descends from the sky
to soothe your souls

the night is not crowded like the day
the night is filled with eternal love
take this night
tights in your arms
as you hold a sweetheart

remember the water of life
is in the dark caverns
don't' be like a big fish
stopping the life's flow
by standing in the mouth of a creek

even mecca is adorned
with black clothes
showing that the heaves
are ready to grace
the human soul

even one prayer
in the mecca of a night
is like a hundred
no one can claim
sleep can build
a temple like this

during a night
the blessed prophet
broke all the idols and
God remained alone
to give equally to all
an endless love

DANCING
THE
FLAME

MY ESSENCE
IS THE ESSENCE

my essence is the essence
of ruby wine
making my chalice
lament in time
cup after cup
wine after wine
the wine gone into my head
and me into the wine

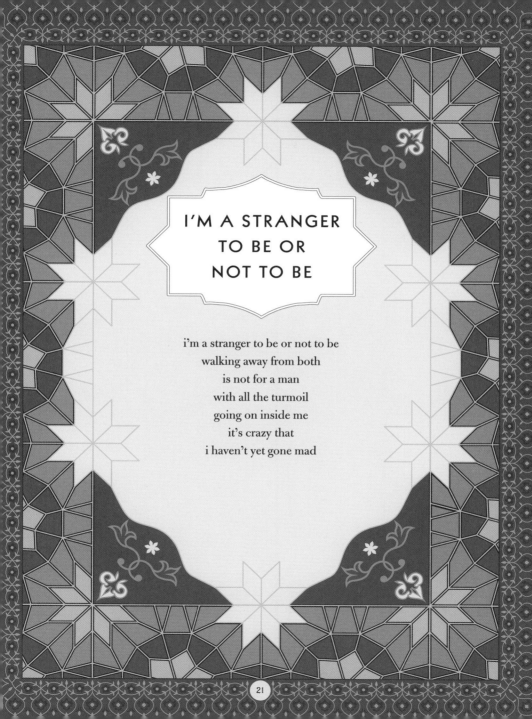

I'M A STRANGER
TO BE OR
NOT TO BE

i'm a stranger to be or not to be
walking away from both
is not for a man
with all the turmoil
going on inside me
it's crazy that
i haven't yet gone mad

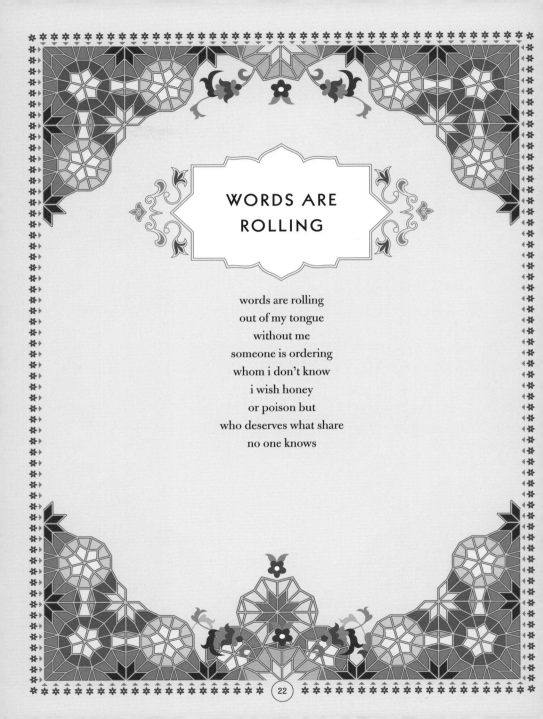

WORDS ARE ROLLING

words are rolling
out of my tongue
without me
someone is ordering
whom i don't know
i wish honey
or poison but
who deserves what share
no one knows

SINCE GOD HAD
WRITTEN MY LIFE

since God had written my life
early in the game
why all the fight and fear
if i were bad
you'll feel relieved
when i'm gone
if i were good
remember
what we have done

MANSOUR WAS THE MAN

Mansour was the man
who said he was God
he merely watched
his body depart
he never said
he was God
it was he who said
he was God

I IMAGINE MARCHING

i imagine marching
to heaven drunk
looking for God
if he is to be found
either my feet
must help me
reach my dream
or i'll lose my head
as i've lost my heart

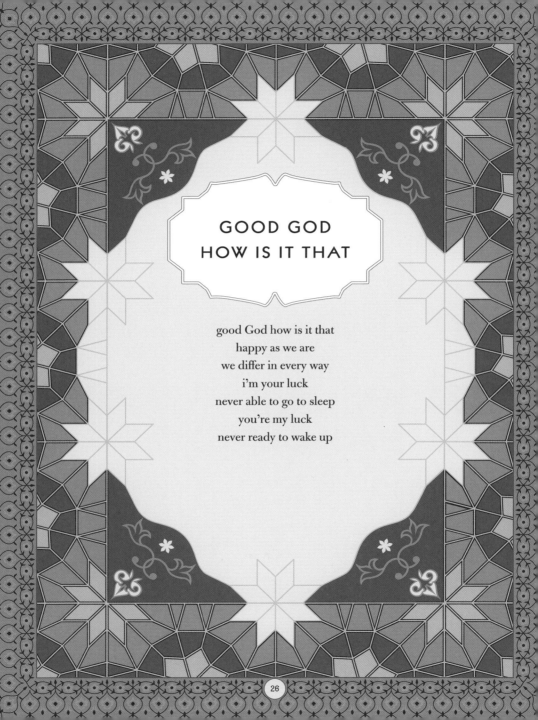

GOOD GOD
HOW IS IT THAT

good God how is it that
happy as we are
we differ in every way
i'm your luck
never able to go to sleep
you're my luck
never ready to wake up

CHILDHOOD PASSED

childhood passed
youth was taken away
from the young
now you're old
get ready for the last flight
every guest has a room
for three days reserved
your three days are up
you should be moving on

AH TEAR DROPS

ah tear drops
brighten my heart
clear the spring blossoms
shinning my sight
flowing one night
remembering only
not any indelicate
moments of my life

ARE YOU A CANDLE

are you a candle
or a free Sufi soul
you have all these six
that show it all
pale and bright
active at night
sleepless
filled with tears
and burning at heart

NIGHT AGAIN

night again
and time to go to sleep
swimming like fish
all day
then sinking deep
next day up again
tending the belongings
i see only God's people
walking his path

WITHOUT
LOOKING AT YOU

without looking at you
i cannot touch the wine
without your hand
i cannot win the dice
you are asking me
to dance from afar
without your music
dance will not arrive

YOU'LL ARRIVE TO

you'll arrive to
the eager hearts
but arrive very late
and when you arrive
like a short breath
that's all you stay
one day you come as a fawn
one day vicious like a lion
like a sword you appear
smooth and soft but
ready to cut

COME ON MESSENGER

come on messenger
don't hide the good news
even if you hang a
prison sign on a garden door
a garden will
not change to a jail

NOW AND THEN

now and then
i hide or show up
now and then
i am Moslem, Jew, or Christian
till my heart becomes
part of every heart
i will appear every day
with a different face

I AM HAPPY
WITH A WINE

i am happy with a wine
that has no cup
i shine every morning
and enjoy myself every night
they say you will
end up with nothing
i am happy
with no end at all

I AM HAPPY WITH

i am happy with
no cloths or money
i am comfortable
when in pain
since i have surrendered
i am happy forever
not half happy
as you are

DON'T RUN AWAY FROM ME

don't run away from me
i'm here to buy you
take a look at me
i'm the light
eager to find you
join me in my work
i'll prosper yours
don't be fed up with me
what i'm selling
is all yours

I AM THE
WHOLE SEA

i am the whole sea
not merely a drop
i am not cross eyes with
prejudice and pride
i express my existence
and every speck of me
cries aloud that
i am not just a particle

UNTIL LAST NIGHT

until last night
i used to complain
calling our separation unfair
i used to be in rage with
this unjust universe
but when i saw you
as only a part of me
with that vision i went
soundly to sleep

I'M NOT FULFILLED

i'm not fulfilled
but i don't want to see
anyone else who is
without touching
the earth at your gate
i don't desire
even the water of life
i have total faith in you
i'm ready to
let go of my life
i am ready to
let go of all other faiths

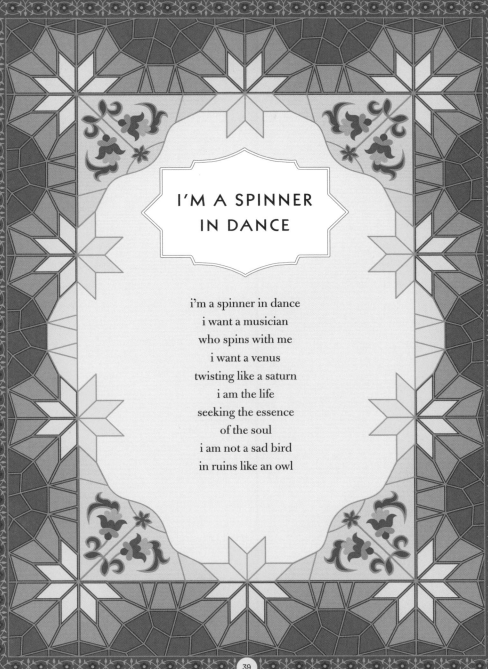

I'M A SPINNER
IN DANCE

i'm a spinner in dance
i want a musician
who spins with me
i want a venus
twisting like a saturn
i am the life
seeking the essence
of the soul
i am not a sad bird
in ruins like an owl

I AM THE ONE WITH HUNGER

i am the one with hunger
but have the happiness of
the one fulfilled
i am a fox who is
filled with lions
i have a self within
fearful of unknown dreams
but don't look at my fears
in essence i'm a brave soul

I'M LIKE SOMEONE WHO IS

i'm like someone who is
riding a marble horse
the one who has
lost the reins in a place
desolate and unknown
like a bird running in panic
to break out of a trap
i wonder where will
this horse of mine
at last be housed

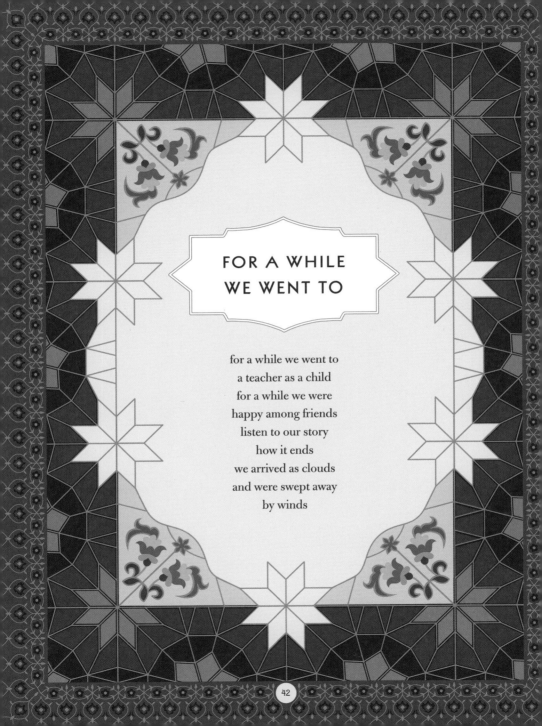

FOR A WHILE
WE WENT TO

for a while we went to
a teacher as a child
for a while we were
happy among friends
listen to our story
how it ends
we arrived as clouds
and were swept away
by winds

TRY YOUR BEST
IN THIS LIFE

try your best in this life
that is the best you can do
when your entire life hangs
on one last breath
it is obvious
there's not much
you can do

YOU'RE CRAWLING
IN A CORNER

you're crawling in a corner
pulling away from the crowd
crying from heavenly troubles
and tired of bitter smiles
if you're a lion
why run away from lions
if you're a vulture
go to find your own kind

CLEAR YOUR
HEART FROM

clear your heart from
jealousy greed and grudge
uproot your bad habits
and bad thoughts
let go of denial
it causes your loss
welcome confession and
your profit will rise

IT IS A WASTE TO PLAY

it is a waste to play
tambourine to the deaf
or lock up a beauty idol
in the house of the blind
it is a waste to push honey
into lips quivering with fever
or force the marriage
of a gay man with a beauty queen

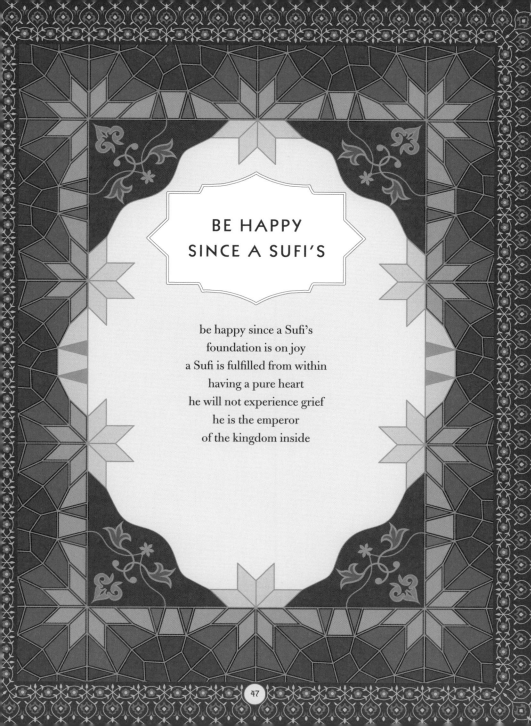

BE HAPPY
SINCE A SUFI'S

be happy since a Sufi's
foundation is on joy
a Sufi is fulfilled from within
having a pure heart
he will not experience grief
he is the emperor
of the kingdom inside

YOU CAN NEVER BREATHE

you can never breathe
healing to your body
till you cut off
worries from your breath
though you're weary at times
surely you can pull through

I'M NOT REALLY ME

i'm not really me
but if for one moment i were
i would scatter this world
like specs of dust
if i were me
with a departed heart
i would uproot myself
like a tree

YOU SAID I'M

you said i'm
irresponsible and mad
i say you must be crazy
expecting me to be wise
you said i have no shame
with a face like steel
yes but steel
acting as a mirror

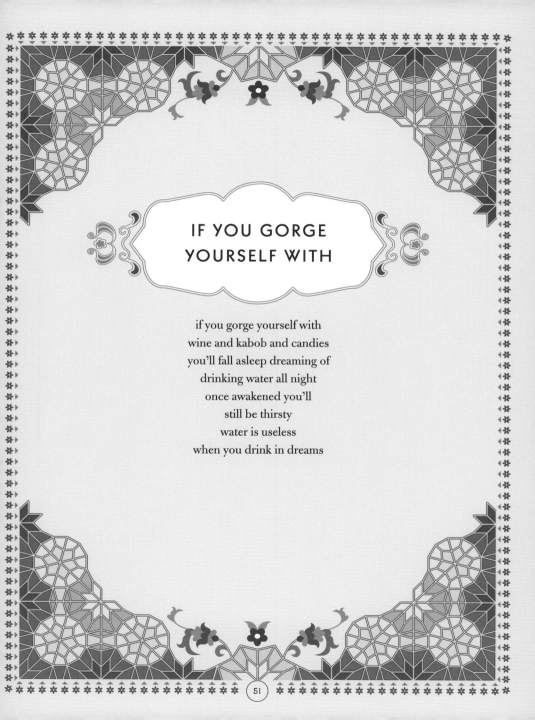

IF YOU GORGE YOURSELF WITH

if you gorge yourself with
wine and kabob and candies
you'll fall asleep dreaming of
drinking water all night
once awakened you'll
still be thirsty
water is useless
when you drink in dreams

IF FOR THE SPAN
OF ONE BREATH

if for the span of one breath
you're allowed a glimpse
of life's secret
you'll let go of
everything at once
but as long as you're
intoxicated with yourself
forever you're fuzzy
fall for the beloved
to be aware and clear

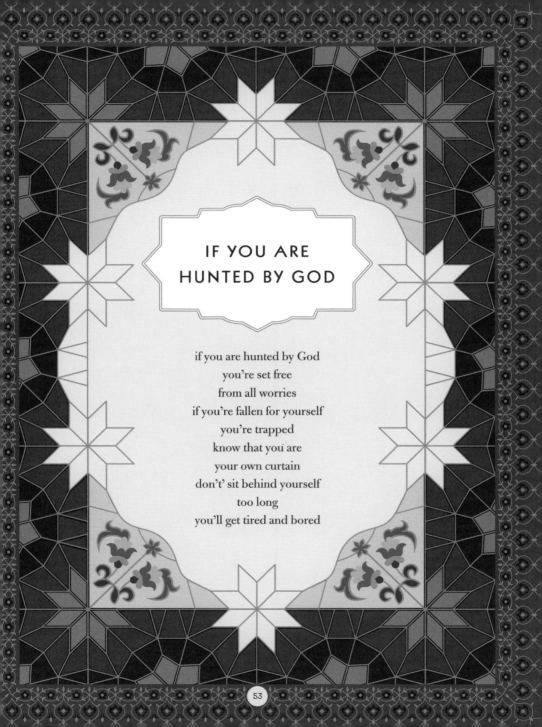

IF YOU ARE
HUNTED BY GOD

if you are hunted by God
you're set free
from all worries
if you're fallen for yourself
you're trapped
know that you are
your own curtain
don't' sit behind yourself
too long
you'll get tired and bored

IF I ONLY KNEW

if i only knew
my own value
and perfection
i would pull out
of this lowly earth
evacuate myself
and rise to
soar my soul
to the ninth heaven

YOU HAVEN'T EXPERIENCED

you haven't experienced
heresy
how can you talk of
faith
you haven't let go of
yourself
how can you talk about the
beloved
you're so busy tending
your lusts
how can you talk about
the soul

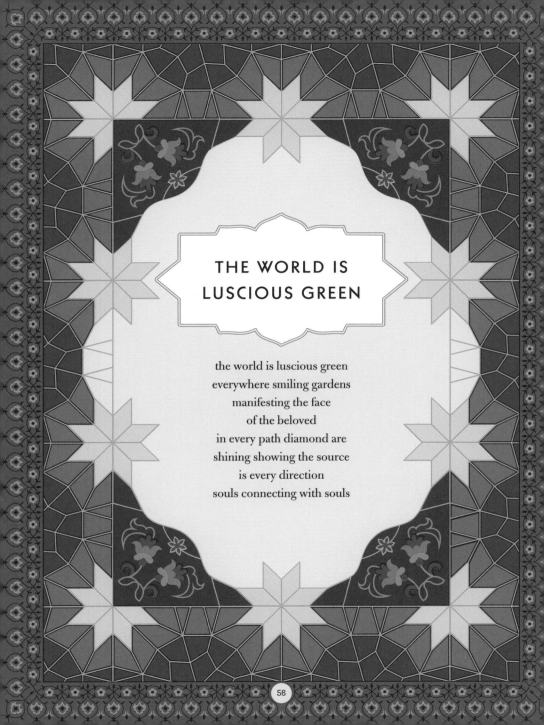

THE WORLD IS LUSCIOUS GREEN

the world is luscious green
everywhere smiling gardens
manifesting the face
of the beloved
in every path diamond are
shining showing the source
is every direction
souls connecting with souls

THE OTHER DAY

the other day
a tender voiced nightingale
sitting by stream
was signing this song
you can make a flower
out of emerald ruby
cumin and gold
but it will have no
aroma of it's own

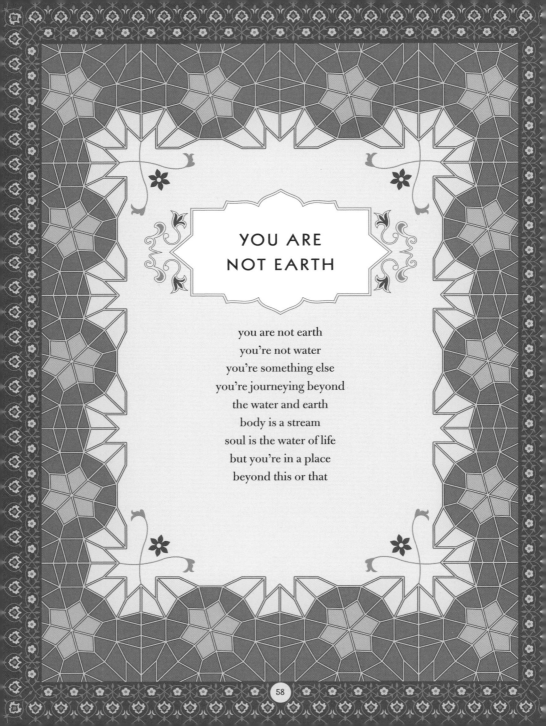

YOU ARE NOT EARTH

you are not earth
you're not water
you're something else
you're journeying beyond
the water and earth
body is a stream
soul is the water of life
but you're in a place
beyond this or that

HOW LONG WILL
YOU WORRY

how long will you worry
about your poor little life
how long will you fret
this stinking world
all you will lose
is this one corpse
if one pile of rubbish
is gone
let go
so what

YOU'RE COMMITTING

you're committing
all the bad deeds
yet you're expecting
good returns
though God is
compassionate and generous
you can't harvest wheat
if you plant barley seeds

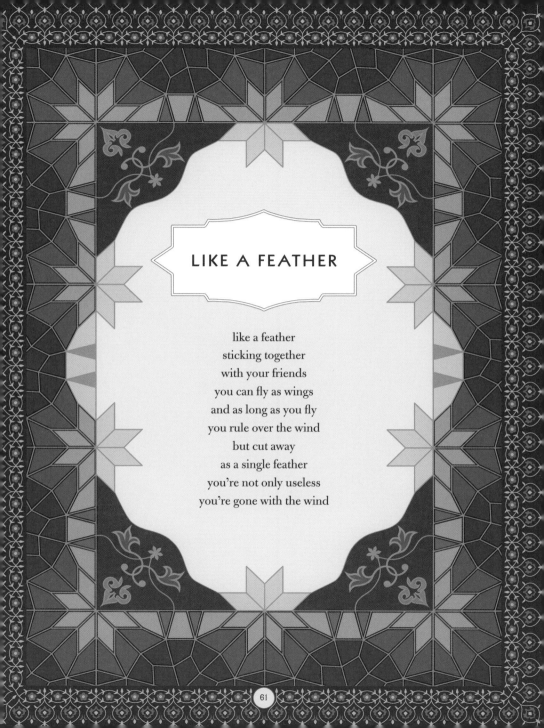

LIKE A FEATHER

like a feather
sticking together
with your friends
you can fly as wings
and as long as you fly
you rule over the wind
but cut away
as a single feather
you're not only useless
you're gone with the wind

MAKE SURE YOU WON'T REGRET

make sure you won't regret
whatever you're done before
like a Sufi never mention
the yesterdays
you belong to the moment
make sure you
won't lose this one breath

ENTER THIS GARDEN

enter this garden
carrying flowers
if you're not all thorns
show your harmony
if you're not a stranger
don't show a poisonous face
if you're not a snake
read this impression
if you're not engraved
yourself on the wall

YOUR HOME IS

your home is
on top of the world
yet you see yourself
as low as the ground
carving your image
only in the earth
while you've left
your real self behind

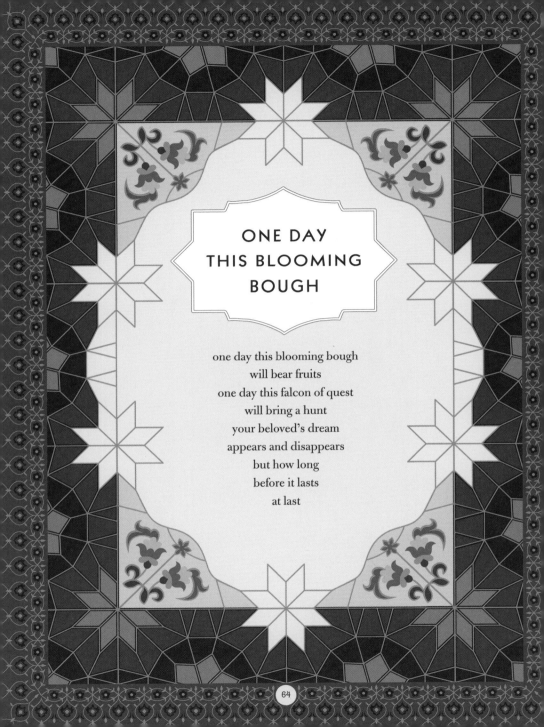

ONE DAY
THIS BLOOMING
BOUGH

one day this blooming bough
will bear fruits
one day this falcon of quest
will bring a hunt
your beloved's dream
appears and disappears
but how long
before it lasts
at last

IF YOU SEEK
THIS WORLD

if you seek this world
you are a mercenary
if you seek paradise
you've lost the truth
if you're happy and carefree
you're excused
since you have never known
the happiness in love's agony

MY DEAR HEART
YOU REALLY

my dear heart you really
never followed God
you never regretted
your wrong doings
you became mystic
and religious
pious and wise
you became everything
but never a Moslem
it yield it all

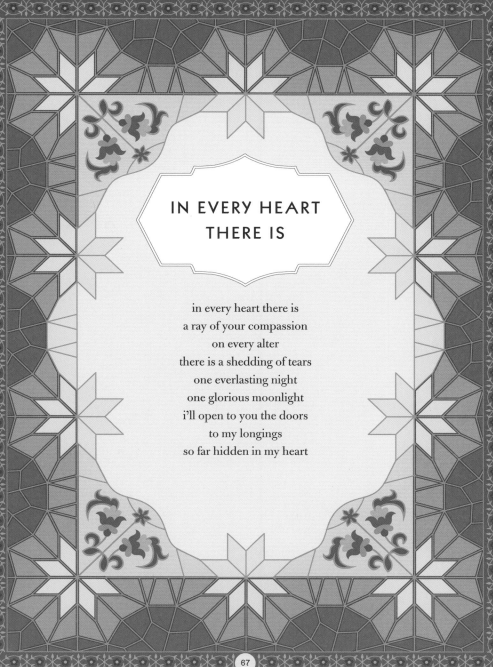

IN EVERY HEART THERE IS

in every heart there is
a ray of your compassion
on every alter
there is a shedding of tears
one everlasting night
one glorious moonlight
i'll open to you the doors
to my longings
so far hidden in my heart

MY GOD YOU ARE A TRAP

my God you are a trap
of a thousand
conspiracies and tricks
my God you've many
mischievous plans
hidden in your head
if the whole world
becomes one stone
i swear to you
my water of life
you will turn it
like a mill stone

IF YOU REALLY KNEW

if you really knew
who was in charge
you would wipe out
ego from your heart
if you really had an insight
not for a moment
would you serve anyone else

THE CRY OF THE VIOL'S MUSIC

the cry of the viol's music
filled with flame
uproar and temptation
the messenger of the desert
to exposer of the
hidden secrets of the heart
where are you coming from

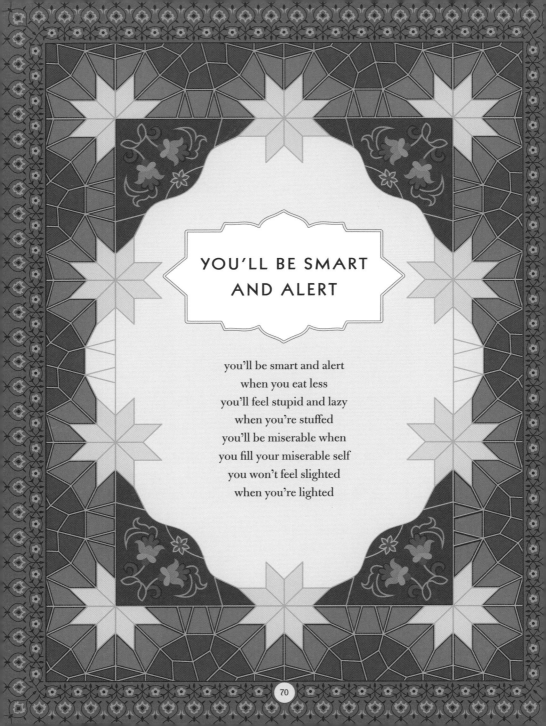

YOU'LL BE SMART
AND ALERT

you'll be smart and alert
when you eat less
you'll feel stupid and lazy
when you're stuffed
you'll be miserable when
you fill your miserable self
you won't feel slighted
when you're lighted

YOU HAVE EYES TO SEE

you have eyes to see
the one who gives you
life and death
the one who makes you
laugh or depressed
that one is everywhere
from your toe to head

WHATEVER MAY HAPPEN

whatever may happen
don't be afraid
come what may
since it won't stay
don't be afraid
savor the moment
and leave what is gone
and fear not
for what may come

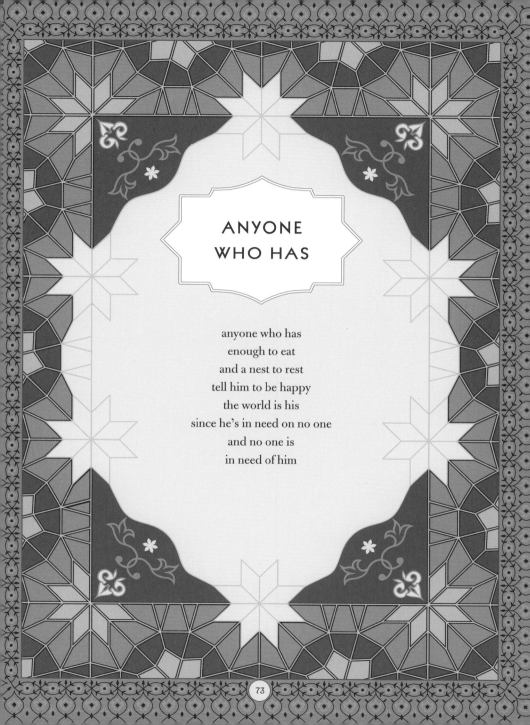

ANYONE WHO HAS

anyone who has
enough to eat
and a nest to rest
tell him to be happy
the world is his
since he's in need on no one
and no one is
in need of him

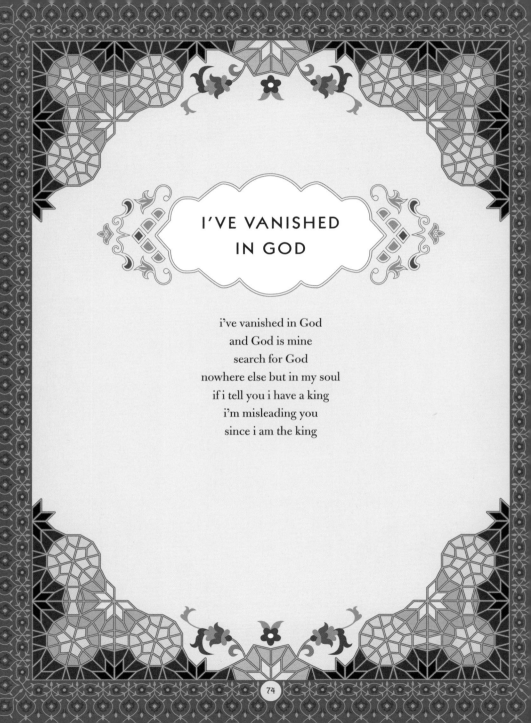

I'VE VANISHED
IN GOD

i've vanished in God
and God is mine
search for God
nowhere else but in my soul
if i tell you i have a king
i'm misleading you
since i am the king

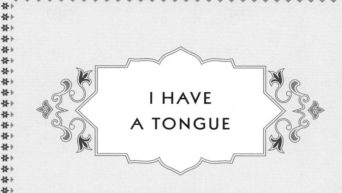

I HAVE A TONGUE

i have a tongue
beside this tongue
i have a hell and paradise
beside the ones you know
free spirited humans are
alive in other's souls
their pure diamond
is from another source

MANY ARE SAD
AND NEVER KNOW

many are sad and never know
where the sorrow comes from
may are happy but ignorant
that it is all from God
many go right and left
not knowing where to go
many me and us are
going on within
but remain unknown

ALL MY LIFE

all my life
my soul's been without me
yet infamous among
female and male
leaving this life and
this world is easy
the difficulty is
bidding you farewell

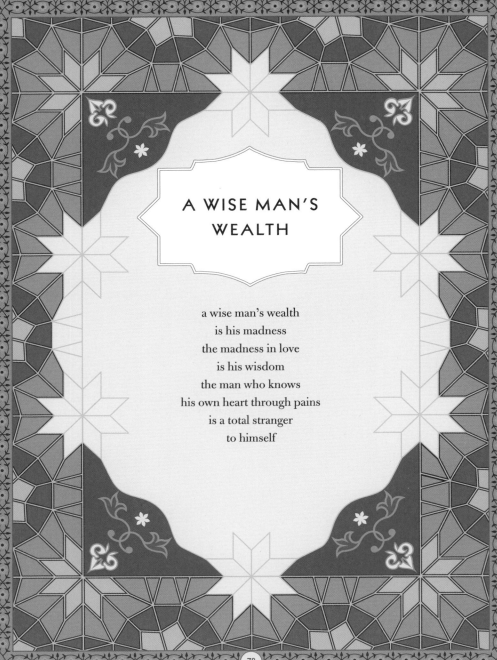

A WISE MAN'S WEALTH

a wise man's wealth
is his madness
the madness in love
is his wisdom
the man who knows
his own heart through pains
is a total stranger
to himself

THERE IS A PASSAGE CONNECTING

there is a passage connecting
our tongue and heart
sustaining the secrets
of the world and soul
as long as our tongue is locked
the channel is open
the moment our tongue unlocks
the passage will close

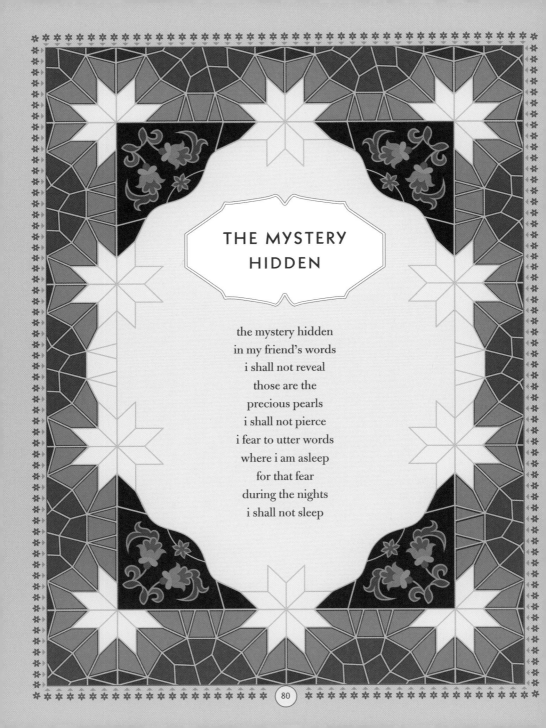

THE MYSTERY
HIDDEN

the mystery hidden
in my friend's words
i shall not reveal
those are the
precious pearls
i shall not pierce
i fear to utter words
where i am asleep
for that fear
during the nights
i shall not sleep

I'VE DRUNK
FROM THE WINE

i've drunk from the wine
whose chalice is the soul
i'm drunk for the one
who enslaved my mind
a candle has arrived
and set me on fire
a candle in whose orbit
turns the mighty sun

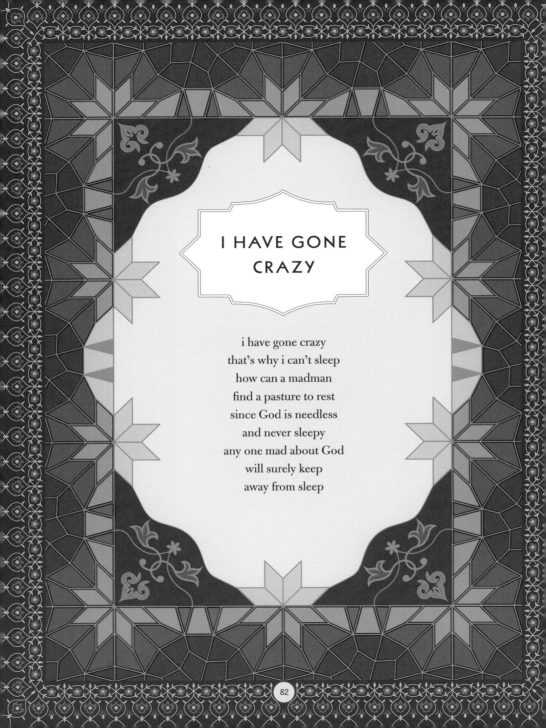

I HAVE GONE CRAZY

i have gone crazy
that's why i can't sleep
how can a madman
find a pasture to rest
since God is needless
and never sleepy
any one mad about God
will surely keep
away from sleep

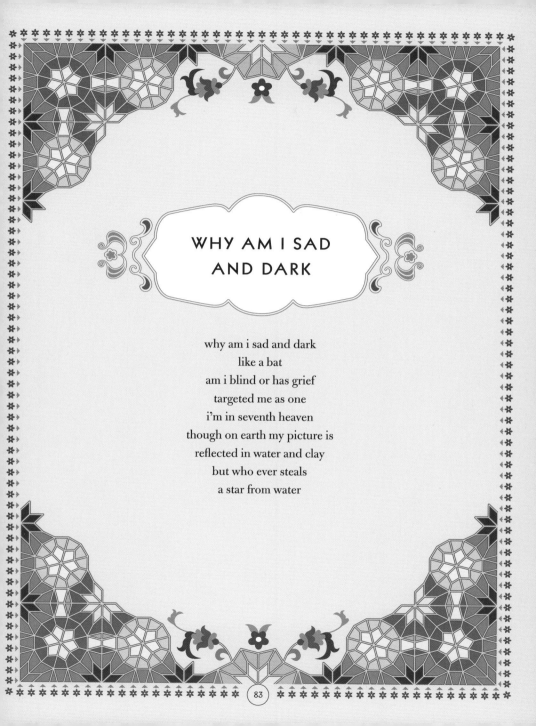

WHY AM I SAD
AND DARK

why am i sad and dark
like a bat
am i blind or has grief
targeted me as one
i'm in seventh heaven
though on earth my picture is
reflected in water and clay
but who ever steals
a star from water

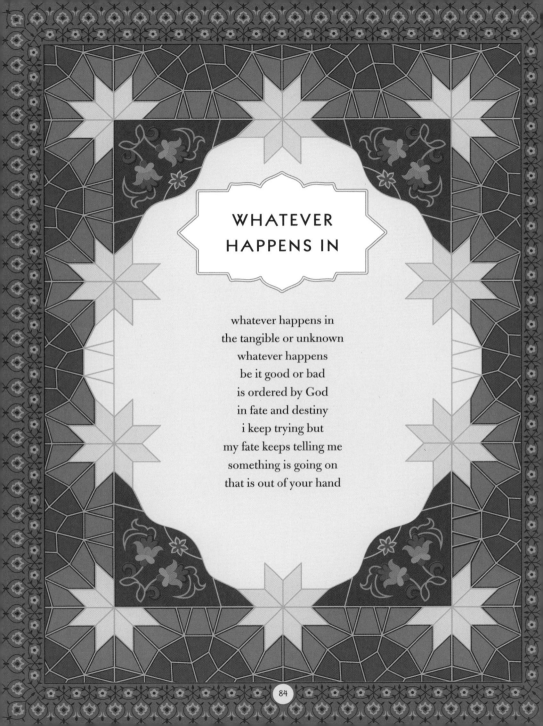

WHATEVER
HAPPENS IN

whatever happens in
the tangible or unknown
whatever happens
be it good or bad
is ordered by God
in fate and destiny
i keep trying but
my fate keeps telling me
something is going on
that is out of your hand

IN THE JOURNEY
OF QUEST

in the journey of quest
the wise and the madman
are the same
in the path of love
the kin and the stranger
are the same
anyone who's been given
the blessings of eternal wine
in his religion
mecca and the shrine of idols
are the same

WHY ARE YOU
SO BITTER

why are you so bitter
aren't you carrying
loads of honey
or are you
loaded with honey
but have no buyer
or is it that
you are incapable
and that's why
you seem confused
or maybe
you're capable but
everything is worthless
in this marketplace

TO KEEP YOU IGNORANT OF

to keep you ignorant of
how conscious the earth is
just like a rabbit
closed eyed yet awake
earth keeps foaming
like a pot
a thousand times
to hide its boiling core

OUT OF THIS WORLD AND OUR LIVES

out of this world and our lives
there is someone
who is nursing us
the one whom we
can never comprehend
i only know this much
we are the shadow
of this one
and the world is
the shadow of us

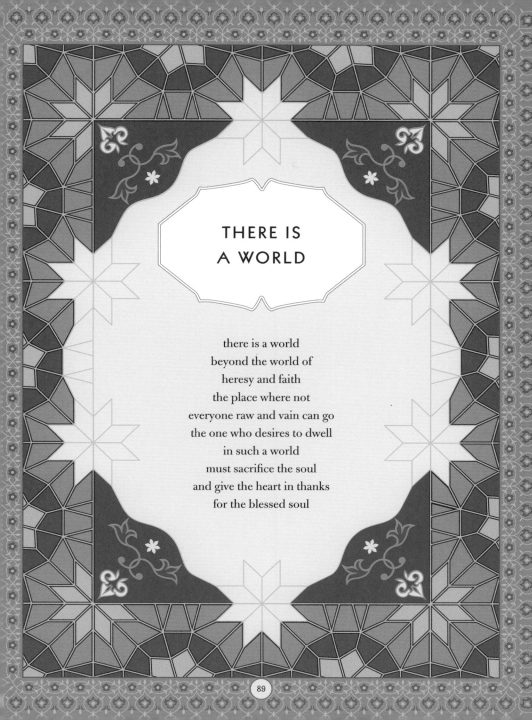

THERE IS
A WORLD

there is a world
beyond the world of
heresy and faith
the place where not
everyone raw and vain can go
the one who desires to dwell
in such a world
must sacrifice the soul
and give the heart in thanks
for the blessed soul

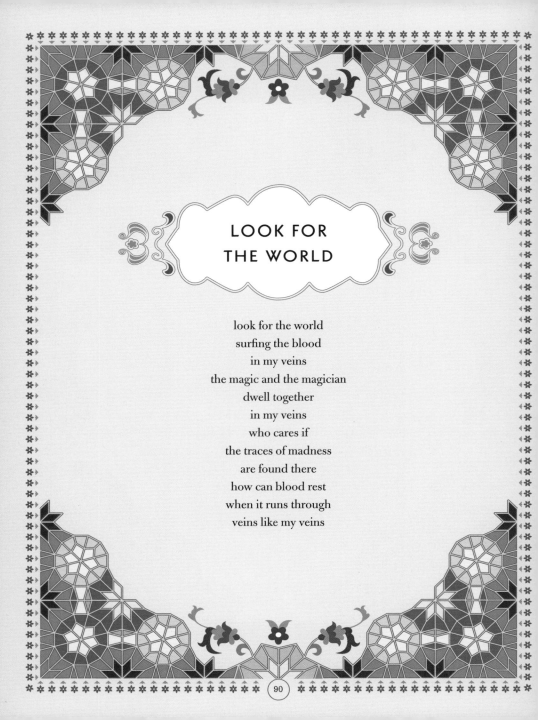

LOOK FOR
THE WORLD

look for the world
surfing the blood
in my veins
the magic and the magician
dwell together
in my veins
who cares if
the traces of madness
are found there
how can blood rest
when it runs through
veins like my veins

FROM THE
START

from the start
i've had a different pact
with eternity
this life of corpses
are separate territories
my dear clergy
you're so proud of
your midnight prayers
there is another dimension
beyond those prayers

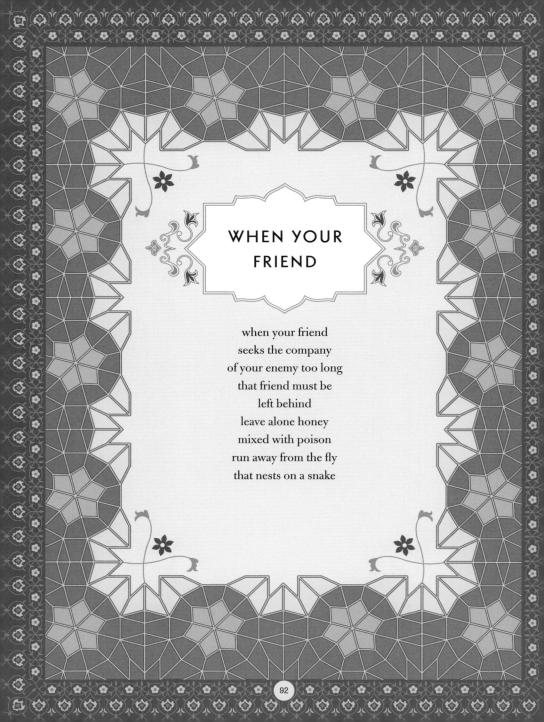

WHEN YOUR FRIEND

when your friend
seeks the company
of your enemy too long
that friend must be
left behind
leave alone honey
mixed with poison
run away from the fly
that nests on a snake

YOU'RE SO STUCK

you're so stuck
with this short-lived life
no one can talk to you
anymore of death
your soul is yearning to arrive
and the home is death
yet your ride
has gone to sleep
somewhere midway

THE PAL
WITHIN YOU

the pal within you
the one who gives you breath
will also give hope
to reach your final quest
up to your last moment
take every breath
from the one inside
who is not playing with you
but generously
endows your every breath

THE ONE YOU KNOW ME

the one you know me
as me it isn't me
who do you think it is
i utter no words
with my tongue
who do you think it is
i'm only a shirt
from my head to my toes
the one whose shirt is me
who do you think it is

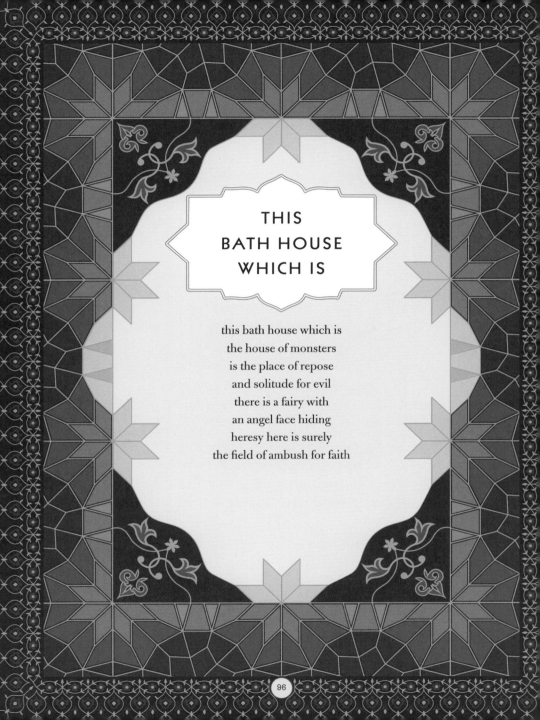

THIS
BATH HOUSE
WHICH IS

this bath house which is
the house of monsters
is the place of repose
and solitude for evil
there is a fairy with
an angel face hiding
heresy here is surely
the field of ambush for faith

THE CERAMIC FORM

the ceramic form
my body
is merely the chalice
of my heart
this wisdom in my thoughts
is the brewing wine
of my heart
all these seeds of knowledge
are nothing but bait
for my heart
and even what i'm
telling you now
is spoken by me
yet it's only a message
from my heart

THIS SPRING
YOU OWN

this spring you own
is not the one everyone seeks
not every water wheel
goes around by stream
not everyone can draw
a far shooting bow
is not everyone's challenge
it takes a hero
not every meager
man can do

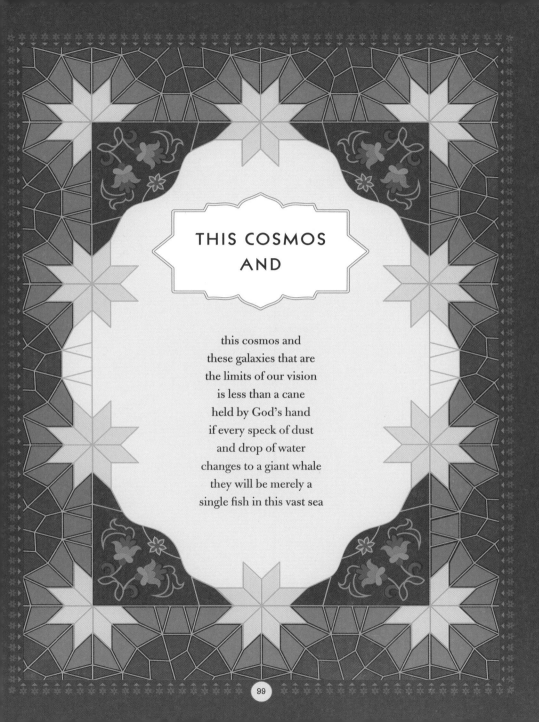

THIS COSMOS AND

this cosmos and
these galaxies that are
the limits of our vision
is less than a cane
held by God's hand
if every speck of dust
and drop of water
changes to a giant whale
they will be merely a
single fish in this vast sea

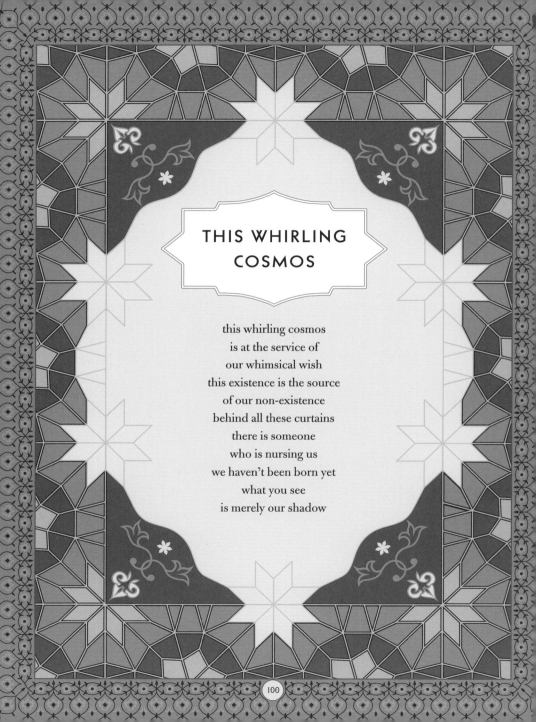

THIS WHIRLING COSMOS

this whirling cosmos
is at the service of
our whimsical wish
this existence is the source
of our non-existence
behind all these curtains
there is someone
who is nursing us
we haven't been born yet
what you see
is merely our shadow

I SAY TO THE NIGHT

i say to the night
if you don't
see me intoxicated
or my sleeplessness
seems exaggerated
it's because my body
is short lived
in this lowly life
while my sleep
has flown away
like an angel
to the heavens

YOU SEE NO CENTER

you see no center
you're so ego ridden
within your shell
your senses are
the brain of your body
and your brain
the sense of your soul
remember
that there is a friend
within your soul
once you surpass
the body sense and soul
there is nothing but friend

ANYONE WHO THINKS

anyone who thinks
heart is what is in the chest
takes only a few steps
and wants the reward to arrive
the prayer rug rosary virtue
confession and repentance
are none but the journey
while everyone
thinks he's already arrived

ANYONE WHO PROMISES YOU

anyone who promises you
help in hard days
beware he only gives
you a free breath
in good times
the whole world
is your friend
but in depressing nights
there are few
with known address

THE ONE WHO HAS

the one who has
a pain but can express
right from the heart
shall rest at ease
but look at this
rare flower blossoming
right within me
i can describe
neither its color nor scent

WHAT IS IT THAT

what is it that
makes our face
shine with pleasure
what is it that when absent
darkens our face
for one moment it
disappears from the face
and in another
appears from an
unknown place

WHAT AM I SUPPOSED TO DO

what am i supposed to do
if my dark night
doesn't want to change
to a bright day
what am i supposed to do
if my luck
doesn't want to
give me a ride
what am i supposed to do
i said once fortune
comes my way
i'll buy up the whole world
but if fortune
gives me no chance
what am i supposed to do

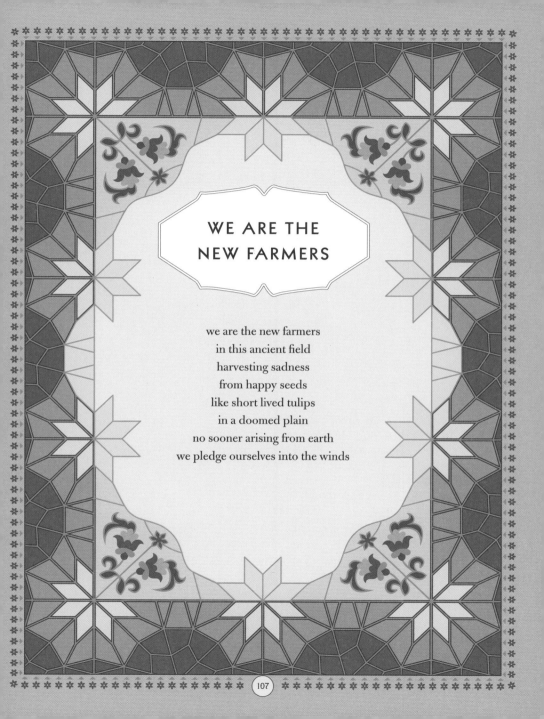

WE ARE THE
NEW FARMERS

we are the new farmers
in this ancient field
harvesting sadness
from happy seeds
like short lived tulips
in a doomed plain
no sooner arising from earth
we pledge ourselves into the winds

HOW CAN ANY HEART

how can any heart
who sees the hidden beauty
be engrossed with
the material of this world
the heart will abandon the eyes
on the day of calling
if it ignores the eternal beauty
and busies itself
with its own soul

ANYONE WHO IS GIVEN

anyone who is given
mind and knowledge
is set up for life
and easy living
but anyone whose head
is left with emptiness
it's been filled
with lots of belongings

WHAT IS THE USE OF LIFE

what is the use of life
or wife or children
for anyone who
has an insight into you
you bestow both worlds
to the one
you first drive insane
once insane what is
the use of
both worlds
to anyone
any more

REMEMBRANCE OF GOD AND

remembrance of God and
a human rises to the absolute
see how splendor arrives
when God shines through
this miraculous ocean
this human inner world
once set in motion
the cry of
"I AM GOD"
will rise and behold

TONIGHT THE WINE BEARER

tonight the wine bearer
passed around the
musk like wine
then stole every heart
and penetrated every faith
pouring wine after wine
causing a storm to rise
unlinking forever
the chains of sanity

I WISH MUCH GRIEF

i wish much grief
for the heart of
any unloyal kind
i wish the vanishing
of any unfaithful friend
no one remembers me
in these times of sadness
except for sorrow
my admired loyal pal

IN TIME OF FASTING

in time of fasting
the earth of your body
changes to gold
like a stone that is
powered for eye-liner
every bite you've eaten
becomes precious as pearls
every moment you've waited
will be diamonds in worth

THIS BEING ALONE

this being alone
is worth more than
a thousand lives around
this freedom
is worth more than
all the estates in the world
to be in solitude
with God
is more precious than
life or belongings
or whatever you've had

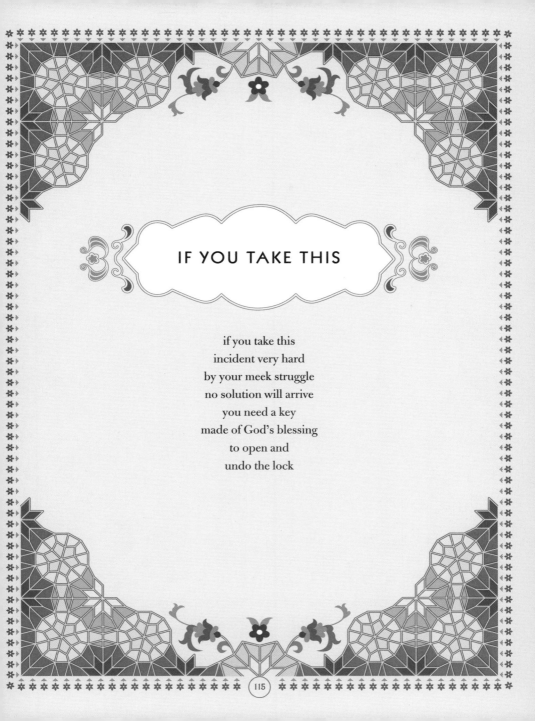

IF YOU TAKE THIS

if you take this
incident very hard
by your meek struggle
no solution will arrive
you need a key
made of God's blessing
to open and
undo the lock

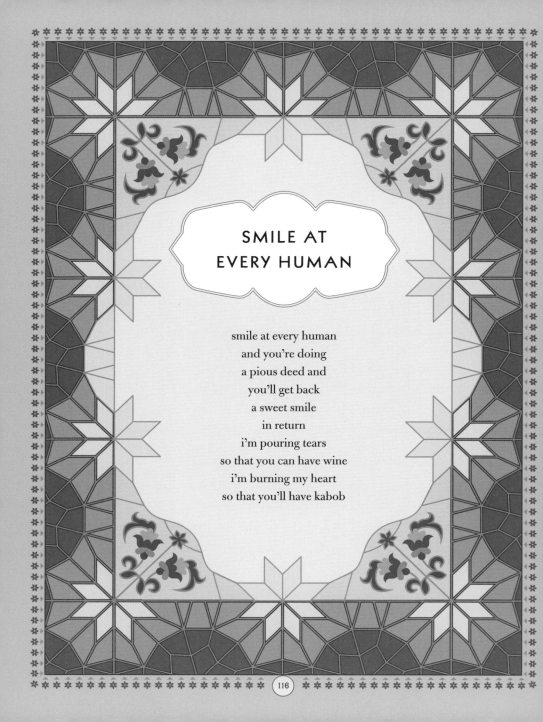

SMILE AT EVERY HUMAN

smile at every human
and you're doing
a pious deed and
you'll get back
a sweet smile
in return
i'm pouring tears
so that you can have wine
i'm burning my heart
so that you'll have kabob

I WISH YOU HAPPINESS

i wish you happiness
and your lips full of smiles
i wish you'd bring
joyous moments
to soul and hearts
of everyone in love
and if anyone sees you
but shows no smile
i wish he'd live like a black pen
dark and confused in life

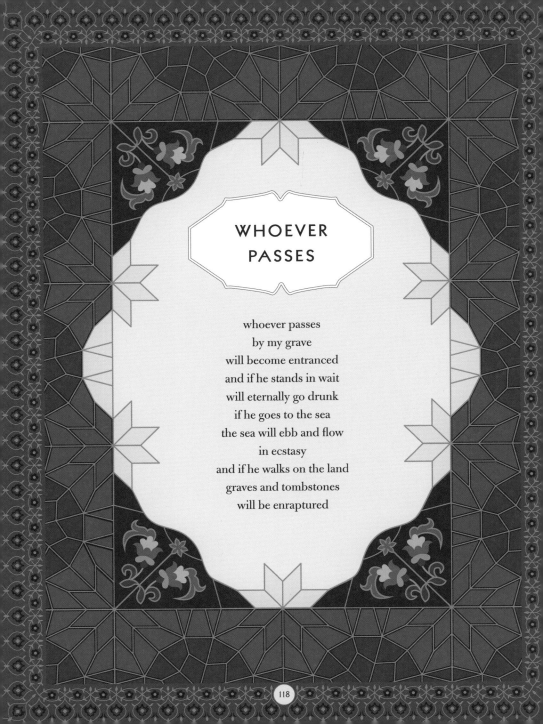

WHOEVER PASSES

whoever passes
by my grave
will become entranced
and if he stands in wait
will eternally go drunk
if he goes to the sea
the sea will ebb and flow
in ecstasy
and if he walks on the land
graves and tombstones
will be enraptured

THIS ISN'T
A REAL DANCE

this isn't a real dance
when you can leap
at any moment
and rise painlessly
like a speck of dust
real dance is when
rise above both worlds
tear your heart away
and are ready to let go
of your life

COME

come
whoever you are
come
come again
even if you are godless
and a worshipper of
fire and idols
come
our home is the home of
never losing hope
come
even if you break
your repentance vows
a hundred times
come again
come

A CANDLE

a candle
spreading light
a mecca
gathering the crowd

I WAS A PIOUS PREACHER

i was a pious preacher
you changed me to a poet
and in me you instilled
rebel rousing and
drunkenness in every feast
i was a solemn
man of sustained prayer
you made me the playing object
of street children

BLESSED IS THE GAMBLER

blessed is the gambler
who has lost everything
except the desire
to gamble
once more

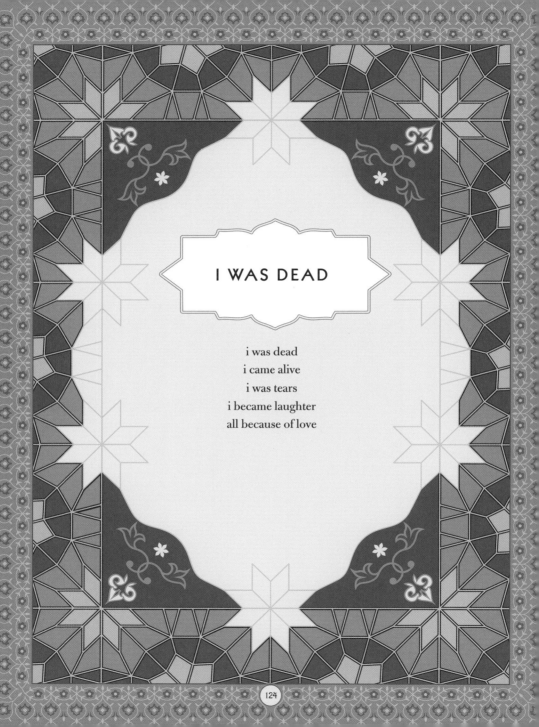

I WAS DEAD

i was dead
i came alive
i was tears
i became laughter
all because of love

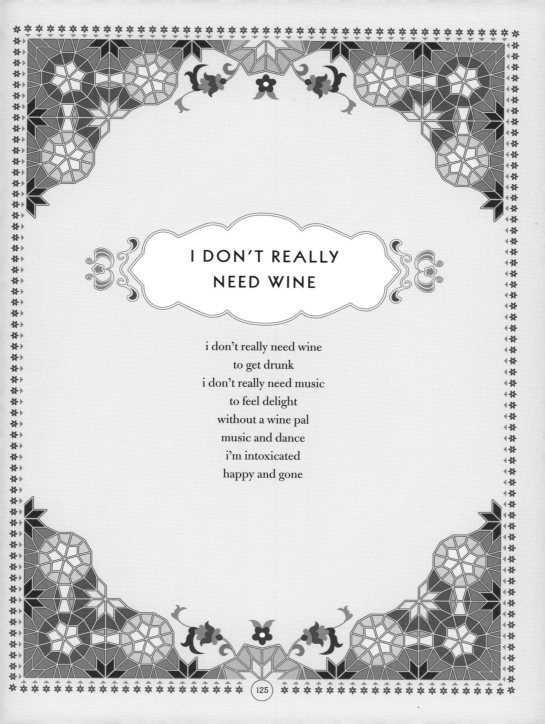

I DON'T REALLY
NEED WINE

i don't really need wine
to get drunk
i don't really need music
to feel delight
without a wine pal
music and dance
i'm intoxicated
happy and gone

COME INSIDE
THE FIRE

come inside the fire
leave your trickery behind
go insane
go mad
burn like a candle-moth